TUESDAY TUCKS ME IN

★ ★ ★

The Loyal Bond between a Soldier and his Service Dog

Fmr. Captain **LUIS CARLOS MONTALVÁN**, USA

with **BRET WITTER** ★ Photographs by **DAN DION**

Roaring Book Press ★ New York

In the morning, every morning,
my friend Luis wakes up to . . .

this.

"Rise and shine,"
  I tell him with a lick.

"The sun is up. It's time!"

Okay, okay, you're right.
Hug first . . .

Then off to the kitchen for my bowl.

Here are your socks, my friend.

And shoes. With just a bit of slobber.

Don't forget your medicine.

"Good boy, Tuesday," Luis laughs. "Good boy."

Luis is a disabled veteran. He went to war, and he came back home in so much pain that he couldn't live a normal life. So I do tasks for him.

I even sleep with him, which helps control his nightmares.

He has daytime nightmares, too, called flashbacks. He gets nervous when people are around . . . or there are sudden movements . . . or loud sounds. That's life in the city, though.

So each morning, we sit together outside our apartment building, waiting, until his breathing and heartbeat tell me he's calm.

Then I walk beside him, always on his right side, so Luis knows that I am there.

And now he takes me everywhere.
To breakfast.
For coffee.
To school.
In cabs.

Yes, even there.

I told you: Luis takes me everywhere.

Every week, we visit the veteran's hospital. Seeing his doctors helps Luis. But sharing me with other veterans helps him, too. He feels like he's giving back.

"Veterans are my pack," he tells me. He means they are his family.

The hospital is stressful, so afterward we reward ourselves with a trip to the park. When my vest is off, I can be a normal dog. I run . . . I chase . . .

I meet friends both furry . . .

. . . and less furry.

Today though, we are
taking the subway—
a serious mission for
a service dog like me.
Luis has trouble with
balance, and he used to
struggle on the stairs.
But now he grabs my
handle and knows that
I am there.

While we wait,
I stand guard.

The subway train
gets crowded.

Very crowded.

Luis doesn't like
crowds. So he hugs
me while we ride.

Usually, the ride is short. But this ride is much longer. What's going on?

"Don't worry, Toopie," Luis says. (Toopie is my nick-name, a combination of "Tuesday" and "Snoopy.")

"Rest for a minute. You're going to like this." Luis always knows how I am feeling. He takes care of me, just like I take care of him.

Finally, "We're here! Come, Tuesday. Come!"
Where are we?

Where?

Where . . . ?

Where . . . ?

Now *this* is a park.

What a day! What a day!
Luis is happy. I am happy.

Now one last thing. Wait . . . yes . . . right there.
Hey, I may be working, but I'm still a dog!

Back home, Luis and I have a quiet dinner.

We watch our favorite videos: dogs, of course.

Answer emails.

Play with toys.

Then, just like every night, Luis brushes me from the top of my head to the tip of my tail. He cleans my ears and wipes my paws.

He even brushes my teeth.
Chicken-flavor toothpaste.
Yum!

Finally, we hug and kiss and say our prayers.

Now I lay me down to sleep,
I pray the Lord my soul to keep.
Angels watch me through the night,
And wake me with the morning light.
Amen.

I know Luis needs me. But he loves me, too. I've heard him say, many times, *I have been brave in my life, but I've been sad, too. I've been afraid, and I've been alone . . . but now when Tuesday tucks me in, I'm happy.*

Because I'm home.

A NOTE ABOUT SERVICE DOGS

TUESDAY IS A SERVICE DOG. Service dogs are trained to help people with disabilities live more independent and happy lives. Tuesday started his training at three days old at an organization called ECAD, Educated Canines Assisting with Disabilities (ecad1.org). When he finished his training two years later, he knew eighty commands. Since I partnered with him in 2008, I have taught him about sixty more. He knows basic commands like "Side"—walk exactly beside a person on the right—and more complicated tasks like turning on lights, opening drawers, and fetching an object out of a room.

My disabilities, including post-traumatic stress disorder (PTSD) and traumatic brain injury (TBI), are the result of war. In 2003, after I was wounded in Iraq, I started to have difficulty sleeping and walking without pain. After my second tour of duty ended in 2006, things got worse. Eventually, I stopped leaving my apartment. I felt angry and ashamed about my conditions, and I withdrew from friends and family. Tuesday saved my life. And dogs like him, trained by wonderful organizations like ECAD, have saved the lives of other veterans, too.

Today, Tuesday and I spend our time visiting disabled veterans and advocating for better treatment of all people with disabilities. I still have difficult days, but Tuesday is always there for me. He listens to my breathing and heartbeat—did you know dogs can hear human heartbeats?—and knows when I am about to have a panic attack. He nuzzles my arm, so that I remember where I am. I try to repay Tuesday's love every day with grooming, petting, and affection. We are best friends, and I would never let anything bad happen to him, just like he would never let anything bad happen to me.

It's hard to be a service dog, just like it's often hard to be disabled. But I would never change who I am or who Tuesday is. Please always respect service dogs and the people who need them. If you want to know more about service dogs, wounded warriors, or ways to help the disabled, please visit the ECAD website or tuesdaytucksmein.com.

With blessings and golden hugs,

Luis & Tuesday

*To Tuesday and the assistance
dogs who help people and
veterans with disabilities*

Text copyright © 2014 by Luis Carlos Montalván and Bret Witter
Photographs copyright © 2014 by Dan Dion
except photograph on page 1 © 2014 Leslie Granda Hill
Published by Roaring Brook Press
Roaring Brook Press is a division of Holtzbrinck Publishing Holdings Limited Partnership
175 Fifth Avenue, New York, New York 10010
mackids.com

Library of Congress Cataloging-in-Publication Data

Montalván, Luis Carlos.
   Tuesday tucks me in : the loyal bond between a soldier and his service dog / Luis Carlos Montalván,
Bret Witter ; [photographs by] Dan Dion.
      pages cm
   Summary: "Based on the *New York Times* bestseller, UNTIL TUESDAY, this full-color picture
book filled with adorable photographs tells the story of the amazing service dog who helps former U.S.
Army Captain Luis Carlos Montalván overcome his combat-related wounds"— Provided by publisher.
   ISBN 978-1-59643-891-0 (hardback)
1. Service dogs—United States.   2. People with disbilities—United States.   3. Human-animal relationships.
I Witter, Bret.   II. TItle.
HV1569.6.M558 2014
362.4'048—dc23
                                                                                        2013032042

Roaring Brook Press books may be purchased for business or promotional use. For information on
bulk purchases please contact Macmillan Corporate and Premium Sales Department at
(800) 221-7945 x5442 or by email at specialmarkets@macmillan.com.

First edition 2014
Book design by Angela Corbo Gier
Printed in China by Toppan Leefung Printing Ltd., Dongguan City, Guangdong Province

3   5   7   9   10   8   6   4